Contents

Five Girls
This is the 2nd edition of this play, the first edition was published in 2021 under the title of Take Three Girls with
ISBN: 9780953279944

The Return of Spring
This is the third edition of this play, originally published in 1996 with
ISBN: 0863194109

The Forest Path
This is the second edition of this play, originally published in 2019 with
ISBN: 9780953279906

Five Girls
a drama

Characters

Emmie
    easily led but basically kind

Bennie
    dominating and thoughtless

Vicky
    kind & understanding

Cally
    falls in love but with consequences

Kate
    rich, intelligent & compassionate

All characters are in their mid to late teens during the passage of the play.

(Five girls appear from different places and stand apart in the dimly lit shadows and in silence. After a while the lights fade to blackout except for one acting area which becomes brightly lit)

EMMIE (approaching and throwing arms around the other) Hi, Bennie. How are you darlin'?

BENNIE (responding likewise) Emmie love, how are you? I'm fine. A bit knackered after a week at college but otherwise O.K. Yeh, fine. Well? You didn't answer. How are you then?

EMMIE Wonderful! Absolutely wonderful! How's the course?

BENNIE O.K., love. O.K.

EMMIE What is it you are doing?

BENNIE Sociology. Hard work at the moment though.

EMMIE No!

BENNIE Absolutely yes! Too much of the 'ology and not enough of the soci' at the moment, petal.

EMMIE Oh! I see. Get your meaning. Too much 'books' and not enough 'looks' eh?

BENNIE Absolutely!

EMMIE Not a man in sight eh?

BENNIE Too many in sight, darling. They just haven't made contact. I feel like a damp firework. Know what I mean?

EMMIE Firework?

BENNIE Yes, absolutely. No-one bothering to come near as nothing will happen in any case.

EMMIE You mean you're....?

BENNIE Oh no dear! Not that. It's just that I can't wait to dry out.

EMMIE Then someone will come to light your touchpaper.

BENNIE And I shall bang like hell.

EMMIE }

BENNIE } (laugh together)

EMMIE You haven't changed a bit, Bennie.

BENNIE I wouldn't wish to dear. One must get one's priorities right mustn't one?

EMMIE Of course.

BENNIE	Soci' first and then 'ology.
EMMIE	Right!
BENNIE	What are you doing with yourself?
EMMIE	Got a place up North. Philosophy.
BENNIE	Really?
EMMIE	Yes. I got the letter yesterday as a matter of fact.
BENNIE	Wonderful! How's your logic then?
EMMIE	My logic's fine. It's my ethics which need brushing up.
BENNIE	Well, if you need any help with that, just ask me.
EMMIE	I don't think your ethics are much to write home about, actually.
BENNIE	}
EMMIE	} (laugh together)
BENNIE	Did you hear about Cally?
EMMIE	No. What is it?
BENNIE	She's pregnant.
EMMIE	No!
BENNIE	It's true.
EMMIE	But she' never been near a man.
BENNIE	Oh it wasn't a man dear. It was Bugs.
EMMIE	Bugs! I didn't think he had it in him.
BENNIE	I don't think that he did either.
EMMIE	Bugs. Well I never! I suppose we'll have to call him Bugs Bunny now.
BENNIE	}
EMMIE	} (laugh together)
BENNIE	That's even funnier than you think. His best friend is Warren.
EMMIE	}
BENNIE	} (laugh together)
VICKY	(joining the other two) You two seem to have a lot to laugh about. Can I join in the fun?
EMMIE	Hi, Vicky. Sure. We were just having a good old gossip about things.
VICKY	What sort of things?
BENNIE	Oh, life in general.

EMMIE	(knowingly) Its meaning.
BENNIE	And the existence of.....
EMMIE	}
BENNIE	} (together) Bugs! (they laugh)
VICKY	Bugs?
EMMIE	(laughing) Yes, Bugs.
VICKY	What about them?
BENNIE	Not them, dear. Him!
VICKY	Him?
BENNIE	Yes him. You know.
EMMIE	Bugs Bunny.
VICKY	Bugs Bunny? (thinks) But I don't like cartoons.
EMMIE	I'm not talking cartoons. I'm talking Mr. Fertilizer.
VICKY	(exasperated) You've lost me.
BENNIE	Cally's pregnant.
VICKY	She's not!
EMMIE	She is.
VICKY	Cally?
EMMIE	Yes.
VICKY	But she never goes near men.
EMMIE	This wasn't a man, dear. It was Bugs.
BENNIE	Bugs Hall.
VICKY	Oh, Bernard! I'm with it now. You mean Bugs ...and Cally...?
EMMIE	That's right.
VICKY	Bugs?
EMMIE	Yep!
VICKY	(starting to laugh) Bugs.......
EMMIE	....and Cally (starting to laugh)
BENNIE	}
EMMIE	} (laugh together)
VICKY	}
VICKY	Well, life is certainly full of little surprises.
BENNIE	Which get bigger everyday.
VICKY	Yes, that's true.
BENNIE	Anyway, Vicky, what are you doing with yourself at the

	moment?
VICKY	Nothing really. I've just left one job and start another on Wednesday week.
BENNIE	What doing?
VICKY	You won't laugh?
BENNIE	Why should I?
VICKY	Well, it's a little strange, that's all.
BENNIE	Why strange?
VICKY	Well, it's at the local Theme Park.
EMMIE	Yes?
VICKY	Conversing with the public.
EMMIE	Yes?
BENNIE	What's strange about that?
VICKY	Wearing a fluffy animal costume.
EMMIE	(puzzled) I see.
BENNIE	So do I. (winks)
EMMIE	}
BENNIE	} (laugh together)
VICKY	Oh don't! It's so embarrassing.
EMMIE	What are you? A bear?
BENNIE	A Fox?
EMMIE	A badger?
BENNIE	A mouse?
VICKY	No, no, no, no, no!
EMMIE	What then?
VICKY	A rabbit.
EMMIE	Rabbit!
BENNIE	Rabbit?
EMMIE	I should watch out for Bugs if I were you.
VICKY	Oh, they are cleaned regularly.
BENNIE	She meant Bugs Hall.
EMMIE	Bugs Bunny!
VICKY	Oh, you...
EMMIE	}
BENNIE	} (laugh together)

VICKY   (thinks about it for a while then laughs too)
(they move off together, still laughing)

(a girl moves into the spotlight and it becomes obvious that she is pregnant)

CALLY   I didn't mean it to happen. Not really. It just did. I'd never been with a boy before. Never touched a boy. Never kissed a boy. Never let a boy do anything to me. Certainly never..... not that. It just happened. I met Bernard in March. He said hello. It was at the dance. The disco. Gemma's. She insisted that I went. 'Get you out of yourself', she said. 'Meet some boys', she said. I didn't really want to meet any boys. Not like that. Oh, I got on all right with them. In conversation. I was always friendly to them. But that's all. They always spoke to me and I always spoke to them. That's all. They were always friendly to me. Yes, I got on with them.... all right. I said hello back. He sat down to talk. I talked. He talked. I talked. We talked. Both of us. I remember smiling. I remember that very well because when I smiled... he smiled. It was a nice smile. His teeth were clean and straight and his skin was clear and shining. Just a hint of darkness at the chin. His nose was straight but not pointed nor thin nor fat. It was straight. And his eyes. Blue. Bright. Sparkling. (pause) He...he touched me. I started away and he said, 'Cally, relax'. I did. I did relax. His hand held mine. It was warm, strong. (pause) It was a nice smile. His eyes were..... blue. His hand held mine firmly. I was drawn to him. He drew me to him. His hand held mine..... strongly. I moved to him. He drew me to him. He pulled me to him. (pause) My head lay on his shoulder. He was still smiling. I was smiling. His hair was brown. Not long. Not short. I don't like short hair. I don't like long hair. I liked his hair. It was...... brown. Blue eyes, brown hair and a smile. The music was playing. I had forgotten to mention that. Well, I suppose there would be music at a dance or a disco. But I was not listening to the music. I was dreaming. Just dreaming. The smile, the eyes, the nose, the hair, (pause) the eyes, the...... smile. His lips touched my forehead. It was nice. They were warm and slightly moist. It was very nice. He held me close, so close. I held him tightly and I was relaxed. Very relaxed. So relaxed. The music played and I ...... dreamed. (pause) Later we left. We walked for miles still holding each other closely. Still smiling. His warm moist lips still close to my forehead. And then ...... it happened. We stopped. He pressed against me. It was nice, so nice. The park was quiet. No-one around. He held me so tight. He kissed me. I kissed him. And then..... it happened. I didn't mean it to happen. Not really. It just did. I'd never been with a boy before. Never touched a boy. Never kissed a boy. Never let a boy do anything to me. Certainly never..... not that. It just happened.

(she moves out of the spotlight as it fades and exits)

(a girl moves into the spotlight as another enters from offstage to join her)

KATE	Vicky! Vicky! ...... Vicky!
VICKY	(recognising her) Kate! I haven't seen you for ages. (they embrace) Where have you been?
KATE	I've been staying in Doncaster for the last few months. At my Gran's place. She invited us up there when Dad's work took him to India and we stayed there until he returned.
VICKY	Doncaster eh? What did you do all that time?
KATE	Oh, went for walks mostly. There's a lot of great countryside around if you know where to look for it. I know Yorkshire is a large place but the buses are pretty good and we did use the youth hostels a bit – Mum and me.
VICKY	Doesn't your Mum work now?
KATE	She did until Dad went but she gave it up so as we could go together. Dad's job in India pays well and he has made sure that we'd plenty to see us through until he returned.
VICKY	Some job eh?
KATE	He's pretty high up now and so money is no problem at all.
VICKY	I wish I could say the same.

KATE	What are you doing?
VICKY	Oh it's just a small job to keep me going until I find my feet.
KATE	Well?
VICKY	It's so embarrassing.
KATE	I won't laugh. Promise.
VICKY	It's at the local Theme Park. I am a helper – talk to the visitors and so on.
KATE	What's wrong with that.
VICKY	I have to dress up.
KATE	I had to wear a uniform when I worked at Lacey's for a year. It's not so bad. You get used to it.
VICKY	Not this uniform I won't.
KATE	Why ever not?
VICKY	It's an animal uniform. A fluffy animal. (pause) A rabbit.
KATE	A rabbit!
VICKY	You promised not to laugh.
KATE	I am not doing. (a smile appears)
VICKY	You promised.
KATE	Oh, Vicky, it's not that bad. At least it pays.
VICKY	Not much.
KATE	What do you mean?
VICKY	The pay is pretty poor.
KATE	How much then?
VICKY	About ninety pounds.
KATE	A week?
VICKY	Yes.
KATE	How many hours?
VICKY	It's about four days a week. Sometimes five.
KATE	How long?
VICKY	About ten hours a day. Sometimes twelve when it's busy.
KATE	That's robbery!
VICKY	I know. But I really need the money. I'm desperate.
KATE	I feel really guilty now.
VICKY	Why?
KATE	For talking to you about my Dad and how he's got lots of

	money and how he supports us and we do all right and we can do what we like and it means that we can travel anywhere and don't have to worry and that when he comes back he going to take us both on a month's tour of China and I didn't tell you that and now I feel worse. I'm sorry.
VICKY	(laughing) It's all right you know, Kate. I don't feel jealous. Not of you. I just feel as I have to work long hours with little reward and that's not your fault.
KATE	I know but …….
VICKY	It's all right you know. I really don't mind. I don't feel jealous of you. I am happy for you. Very happy. And I tell you this – it is absolutely wonderful to see you again. Really wonderful. I have missed you.
KATE	Oh, Vicky. Thanks. (they embrace) Thanks, I've missed you too.
VICKY	(pause) Have you heard about Cally?
KATE	No. What is it.
VICKY	She's …..
KATE	I know ….. found a boy!
VICKY	You're very warm.
KATE	A girl?
VICKY }	
KATE	} (together they laugh)
VICKY	Actually you have gone a little cooler.
KATE	Perhaps she's found a *real* man?
VICKY	That is pretty hot, Kate. But I don't think that you're going to get it. Not this side of Christmas at least.
KATE	What is it then?
VICKY	She's pregnant.
KATE	What?
VICKY	It's true. Every word of it.
KATE	But….
VICKY	I know. Everyone says that. At least if you're going to say what I think. The fact is it's true. No-one believes it but it is the absolute Gospel truth. And come to think of it you don't

	need to have anyone's word as proof because... come to think of it it's rather obvious now.
KATE	When?
VICKY	She's around five months. And big for her time.
KATE	I shall have to see her.
VICKY	She's very unhappy. Desperately unhappy.
KATE	Didn't she want it?
VICKY	I don't know.
KATE	But if she's unhappy I can't think why she's keeping it.
VICKY	I just think that she feels ever so guilty about getting herself into this situation in the first place. She can't handle the shock. She didn't believe herself that it would happen, that it could happen. But it did and now she has to cope in the best way she can. She is speaking to very few people. She won't talk to Bennie or Emmie at all. She did speak to me. But you have to show understanding, compassion, sympathy. You can't treat her in any other way. If you do, then I for one cannot tell how she might react. She might have a breakdown. She might turn violent.
KATE	But she's not that type.
VICKY	Wasn't. But who knows. She's different. She is depressed and desperately, desperately unhappy.
KATE	Poor Cally.
VICKY	Yes, poor Cally.
KATE	(pause) I must see her.
VICKY	Take it easy. (puts her arm on Kate's shoulder)
KATE	Yes of course.
VICKY	(pause) Well?
KATE	Yes. I'll go now. I understand what you've said. I'll be very careful. And very kind. (she moves to go)
VICKY	Kate!
KATE	Yes?
VICKY	I know you will. I know you will.
KATE	(smiles) See you.
VICKY	Yes. See you.

(they move off in different directions)

(a girl enters the spotlight - in the background a dim light illuminates Bennie who watches)

EMMIE Bennie and I spoke to Cally the other day. The little shit. We asked after her. Said how wonderful we thought the news was – of her having the baby like – and that we hoped it would grow big and strong just like Bugs. She told us to piss off. Piss off, she said. I ask you. You express your congratulations and are treated like dirt. It makes you sick. Bennie was furious. Well I was as well but Bennie got really angry and told her she hoped it would be triplets. I thought that was a bit over the top but, well, she was treating us like dirt. After our kind words too. Bennie threw some insults after that. Bennie always gets hot under the collar. She's quick tempered and can be rather abusive but, well, I suppose Cally deserved it. What with our being so delighted at her condition, I cannot understand why Cally didn't just say thanks. She even gave me the impression that she didn't want the baby, didn't care about the baby. I mean babies are wonderful things and they should be appreciated. I wouldn't want one of course. Not yet. I like a bit of fun but, well, you have to be careful. Very careful these days. So we left. Cally said she didn't want to speak to us again and Bennie said that was great because she had never liked her in the first place. Piss off, Cally said. I can't tell you what Bennie said. Even I don't say those things. In any case I think I still like Cally. I think so. (pause) As we left I turned to look back at Cally. She was crying. I felt my eyes start to water and I looked at her for several seconds and then Bennie called me. I followed Bennie. I felt sad all of a sudden. Very sad. She shouldn't have cried. (pause) Bennie soon made me feel better. She told some of her stories and we had a good laugh. A good laugh. (pause - the light fades on Bennie) I still think about Cally. I think about Cally a lot. Perhaps I wasn't very kind when I come to think of it. Cally is really very sweet.

(she moves off)

(two girls enter the spotlight)

KATE	I had to come.
CALLY	Why?
KATE	To see you.
CALLY	To laugh?
KATE	Laugh?
CALLY	Everyone else does.
KATE	Everyone?
CALLY	Nearly.
KATE	Not Vicky.
CALLY	(pause) No. Not Vicky.
KATE	Who then?
CALLY	Bennie. Emmie.
KATE	Emmie?
CALLY	And Bennie.
KATE	I can understand that. But not Emmie.
CALLY	Not as bad.
KATE	Bennie is too bossy. Emmie tries to be like her but she isn't. Not really. She is basically very nice but very easily led.
CALLY	I told them to piss off.
KATE	That's not like you.
CALLY	I know. I don't think it was me speaking. It just came out. Just like that.
KATE	I can understand why.
CALLY	They hoped my baby would be all right. My baby. Huh! How strange that sounds. They were gloating over my condition. You could see that in their faces. Both of them. Well, especially Bennie's. Emmie…. Well…. I never really saw her face. I just felt that they were both laughing. At me. Both of them. I do hope it will be big and strong like Bugs, they said. Bugs… Bernard … isn't big and strong. He is nice and I like

	him but he is not like they suggested. He is just nice. I like him. I like to hold him. His lovely brown hair. His blue eyes. I like him very much. He is not big and strong. He is warm. He has a lovely smile and I like him very much and (breaks down) I love him and I don't want this baby. I wanted his love but not this.
KATE	Oh, Cally! (embraces her)
CALLY	(crying) I really am in love with him, Kate.
KATE	I know.
CALLY	(recovering a little) So they left me … Bennie and Emmie. They left me. I cried after that. I felt someone looking at me and I turned my head a little and saw Emmie, in the distance, looking at me. I think she looked very sad. I think she may have cried a little. I think she knew how I felt. (pause) Yes, I think she did.
KATE	I think you may be right, Cally. If I know Emmie at all.
CALLY	I spoke to Vicky the other day. I told her how I felt. I think she understands. I know she understands. Like you Kate. You understand don't you?
KATE	(smiles) Yes, Cally. I understand.
CALLY	I'd hoped that you would. You're not like Bennie …. or Emmie for that matter. Bennie doesn't understand anything. And Emmie …(pause) … I don't know. Perhaps she does understand and doesn't want to admit it. To herself maybe … but especially to Bennie. I don't think that Bennie would like it if she thought that Emmie was in the least sympathetic. I wish Emmie would think for herself … like you …. and Vicky. I wish she would.
KATE	(pause) Cally?
CALLY	Yes.
KATE	I think…….. well I …..(pause)
CALLY	What do you think?
KATE	Oh I don't know.
CALLY	Please?
KATE	(pause) I think that Emmie really does understand. I think

	she wants to understand. I know that Bennie influences her a lot but I really do think that Emmie is beginning to realize that Bennie is not the best thing for her.
CALLY	Do you really?
KATE	I also think that Emmie really wants you to be happy. Not like Bennie.
CALLY	Do you?
KATE	And …..(pause) ….. and …..
CALLY	Well?
KATE	And I think that Emmie is jealous of you.
CALLY	Jealous?
KATE	Yes, jealous.
CALLY	But how? Why?
KATE	Well, because she loves children. Really loves them. I think that she can't wait to get married and have some. Oh, I'm sorry, Cally. I didn't mean to mention marriage.
CALLY	That's all right, Kate. I know what you mean. But do you think that she's really jealous?
KATE	Really.
CALLY	Perhaps that's why she appeared to be rude to me when she was with Bennie.
KATE	Oh no. I don't think so. I think that was really Bennie speaking. Not Emmie. You know how it is with Bennie. She has to control every conversation, every relationship every…. Well, doesn't she?
CALLY	Yes, you're right, of course. I wonder what was really going on in Emmie's mind.

(a spotlight fades up on Emmie as the others fade a little)

EMMIE	(bewildered) I thought I knew myself. I thought I really knew myself. But I don't. Not any more. When I spoke to Cally the other day. And when Bennie did too. Cally turned on us and told us to piss off. Cally never swears. Afterwards it made me think. It made me think hard … very hard. Perhaps I didn't know myself after all. I would never hurt anyone's feelings. I

like to laugh. Well everyone does, don't they? Well? Don't they? But I don't like to see anyone hurt. I really like Cally. I wouldn't want to hurt her. Especially now, when she's pregnant. (pause) It must be nice to have a child of your own. Not now, I mean, but when you're married. It must be nice to be married. It must be nice to have children. You'd have someone to take special care of. Not just one, of course, there would be your husband as well. Husband! It's a funny word isn't it? Husband! Husband! (pause) Husband! Someone to love. And children to take care of and love. Mmmm! (pause) I think I understand Cally... what she is going through. Yes, I am sure that I do. Husband! Children! (pause) I think I'm jealous of her really – Cally. Yes, jealous.
(Lights fade to blackout)

(Light up)

VICKY	Hi there!
KATE	Hi! I saw Cally.
VICKY	Really? How is she?
KATE	Much as you said, at first.
VICKY	At first?
KATE	Yes. We talked it though. We talked about Emmie and Bennie (pause) and you.
VICKY	Me?
KATE	Just a little. She likes you, Vicky. She knows that you understand. That you care.
VICKY	I'm glad.
KATE	And we talked about Emmie.
VICKY	And?
KATE	Well, I explained about Emmie. What I thought, and so on.
VICKY	And?
KATE	And how I thought that Emmie was actually jealous of Cally.
VICKY	Mmm?

KATE And I think that Cally understands Emmie as well. She realizes that Bennie influences her too much. And that Emmie is really a one hundred per

	cent nice girl but that Bennie is a much stronger character and, well, forces her to behave in the way that she does.
VICKY	I'm glad about that. I'm really glad. Bennie can be such a….
KATE	(cutting in) Cally knows that. She really does understand.
VICKY	(pause) Good.
KATE	(pause) Look, do you think I should speak to Bennie?
VICKY	Why?
KATE	To explain how Cally feels.
VICKY	That wouldn't do any good. I am sure that Bennie knows how Cally feels but just doesn't care.
KATE	Do you really? Do you really think that Bennie is uncaring? I know that she is bossy. I know that she is hurtful at times and appears not to care how she affects others' feelings, but I cannot believe that there is no good in her at all.
VICKY	You might be right but I have never seen the good side of her. Not ever. I am friendly with her, oh yes! I daren't not be. She is one of those individuals whom it is better to have on your side rather than against you. And she does speak before she thinks much of the time. But I have never seen a caring side to her. Not ever.
KATE	I still think that I would like to talk to her. Just to see if she really does care about people. Cally in particular.
VICKY	Well I can't stop you. I really do hope that you have some success. Make her see that she hurts people. That making fun of people is not always fun for everyone. That…
KATE	I'll try.
VICKY	(pause) Okay! I wish you luck.

(Lights fade to blackout)

(A girl joins another in the spotlight)

EMMIE	Cally! Cally, I am really sorry about the other day. When I was with Bennie.
CALLY	(pause) I don't want this baby you know. I just don't want it.
EMMIE	Don't want it? Why ever not?
CALLY	Why should I tell you? After what you said to me!

EMMIE	It wasn't me you know, Cally. It wasn't me.
CALLY	Bennie said things. You were with Bennie. You agreed with her.
EMMIE	I didn't. I didn't agree with her.
CALLY	Why were you with her then? (pause) (tearfully) I know. (pause) I saw you leave, following Bennie. You looked back at me. You were crying. You must have felt something.
EMMIE	You're right. I did cry. I thought Bennie went too far. I do understand how you feel. I did then. A little. But I understand more now. A lot more.
CALLY	I really believe you do, Emmie. I really believe you do (pause) Thank you for coming, Emmie. I do appreciate it. I just wish Bennie would understand. I wish she wasn't so cruel, so uncaring, so arrogant.
EMMIE	Maybe she'll change one day.
CALLY	I don't think so. She has always been like it. Ever since I can remember.
EMMIE	Me too. But people do change, Cally. I don't think we should give up hope that she might change. You never know.
CALLY	Perhaps.
EMMIE	(puts hand on Cally's shoulder and moves to leave) You never know.
CALLY	(smiles)

(Lights fade to blackout)

(Two girls talk in the spotlight)

BENNIE	She's a little shit. She told me to piss off. Why should I treat her properly? Just tell me that.
KATE	Why do you think she said those things? Why?
BENNIE	How should I know? Should I care? I only asked how she was and hoped the baby was all right. She told me to piss off. Is that the way to talk to people?
KATE	Did you ever stop to ask yourself why she said 'piss off'? Did you?
BENNIE	Why should I? I was only being friendly. There was no

	reason for her to…
KATE	Bennie! Think for once will you? For once in your life try to imagine how someone else is feeling. Can you imagine what Cally has been through? Can you imagine what she is going through? Every second of every minute of every hour of every day she thinks only of that baby. She thinks of that baby. And why? Why does she spend all of the time thinking about that baby. I'll tell you. It is because it is something or someone that she does not want. She does not wish to be associated with. She does not want to have that baby, Bennie! She does not want the baby!
BENNIE	She…
KATE	Let me finish. Why do you think she does not want that baby? Why, tell me? She has met a boy, Bernard. For the first time in her life she has met a boy who she can talk to, smile with, laugh with embrace and make love to. When she did that (pause) for the first time in her life, when she did that (pause) she is landed with someone else to think about, someone else to worry about, someone else to love. For God's sake Bennie! She is sixteen years old and she does not want the baby. She does not want it! She wants her youth. She wants her life. She wants her love. She loves Bernard.
BENNIE	(pause) (Bennie is moved by this speech) I don't know what to say. Kate? For the first time in my life I do not know what to say. (pause) What can I do? How can I say sorry? I do want to say sorry. I really do. (pause) Help me Kate. (cries) Help me!
KATE	Oh, Bennie. Just tell her. Tell Cally you're sorry. She'll understand. I know that she'll understand.
BENNIE	Maybe, Kate. Maybe. (pause) I know. I know what to do.

(lights fade to blackout)

(lights fade up on a group of three girls)

KATE	…and she left me. She was truly very sorry. I am sure of it.

VICKY	Well it surprises me but, well, Kate you should take all of the credit. No-one else could have made her see how she was wrong. No-one could have made her understand how cruel she had been.
EMMIE	Well done, Kate. Thank you.
KATE	It wasn't me. I was only part of it. When I spoke to her I had to talk to her about you two. You two as her friends. She had to know and understand how you both felt. Not only me. She saw you, Emmie, that day Cally told you to piss off. She saw you wait a little as you left Cally. Wait and look back with a small tear in your eye. She understands now why you felt that way.
EMMIE	But…..
KATE	And you Vicky. She had realized quite some time ago that you didn't really like her. That you spoke to her and kept friends with her to avoid aggravation. But you did not like her.
VICKY	Why is she always so dominating? So aggressive sometimes?
KATE	She doesn't want to lose anything or anybody. She needs people and the only way she felt she could keep people is by making people rely on her. Follow her. She had to feel that she was in control.
EMMIE	I don't understand.
KATE	And why should you? What you probably did not know was that her parents separated when she was a lot younger. No-one would take responsibility for her and she was left alone for three days in her house until a neighbour found her. Well to cut a long story short, since that time she has been living with foster parents. They love her, yes. But it is not the same as having your own parents. Parents who share the same blood and love you and care for you as if you were part of them.
EMMIE	I see. I didn't know.
KATE	There is no reason why you should have done. I only found out when she told me in a fit of tears. After our, well, our little

	talk.
VICKY	You deserve a medal, Kate.
KATE	No. I deserve nothing. I would not have found out at all if each of you had not behaved emotionally or strangely at times. It made her think. It really did make her think. So you see, it was not only me. I helped by having a go at her. Trying to get her to see and understand. But it was not only me. It would not have been possible if it was only me. It was both of you as well. It had to be to make her really understand. It had to take three girls.

(lights fade to blackout)

(there is a sound of a car screeching to a halt - a thump - a scream – in a bright white light Cally is seen to collapse on the ground)

(lights fade up)

BENNIE	(sitting) I thought about it a lot. After what Kate had said to me that night. She was right. I don't know how or why I did not see it before. I have been cruel, heartless and a fool. To think that I should admit that! That I should admit to being a fool! (pause) When Emmie turned back that day to look at Cally I knew that something was not right. Something in me. She cried, I know that she cried. It seems strange for me to say this but that made me hurt inside. Like I never hurt before. I could still not accept that it was me that was wrong. Then there was Vicky. She always looked at me strangely. She never argued with me but you could see that she did not always like what I did. I did not know then why that was but now…. (pause) I know now. Kate made me realize that. I suppose that I have a lot to thank Kate for. (pause) I wanted to repair the damage that I had done. I wanted to talk to Cally, make friends with Cally, be with Cally. Be with Cally's child. (cries) (pause) I went to the toyshop, the big one in the High Street. I was there hours. I wanted what I chose for Cally, for Cally's baby to be the best – the very best. It was

too. It was large and pink and fluffy with a lovely smile. I knew that she would like it. Cally… And the baby. (pause) When the accident happened I saw her fall to the ground. She was hurt. Hurt badly. She gripped her stomach and I knew that she was in pain. (pause) She died within a few hours. The baby. Aborted at six months. Not a chance. (pause) Cally recovered physically from event the but she will never forget that day. The day that her child died. (pause) You see it was the shock of the accident she saw that caused it to happen. Poor Cally. Even though she did not want it in the first place, after six months it is very much a part of you. I would have loved it as well. My time for love has passed. (pause) I came out of the toyshop, walked along the High Street towards St Gregory's Lane. The pink and happy fluffiness smiling out of the top of the bag. Just as I reached the middle of the road this car came round the corner like a bat out of hell. Drunk he was. Doing sixty in a built-up area. (pause) I didn't feel a thing when the car hit me. My last thought was for Cally's baby. Cally's little baby. (pause) She never did get the toy. It lay lifeless and flat beside me just as I lay lifeless and flat beside the toy in a pool of blood….. My blood. (pause) From this place, where there is no pain, no hurt, I can see everything now. (stands) I can understand everything. Love everything. Even Cally's baby.

(lights fade to blackout)

THE END

The Return of Spring
a drama

Characters

Geoff
      Father
Ginny
      Daughter
Ellie
      Mother
Mary
      Ginny's sister
Rick
      Ginny's boyfriend

Ellie, Geoff, Ginny and Mary were a close family until Ginny met Rick, then her relationship with the family started to turn sour. Independence alone was what she wanted and Rick gave her that freedom. On realising her own attitude was selfish and that Rick only wanted from her what he could get, Ginny finally returned to loving her family.

This play was first performed in Norfolk in 1996.

(Lx pool on GEOFF)

GEOFF It's Autumn now. Spring was a such a long time ago - it seems like a hundred years. Flowers were bright and gay; the primary colours intense against the haze and still against the backdrop of the afternoon sky. Birds sang. Swallows swooped and the kestrels hung motionless awaiting the appearance of their insignificant prey. Then the breezes came and at first were gentle; leaves chattered their way through their youth until their voices broke. Ginny was pale, but bright of spirit. She even wore clothes which contradicted her complexion. She was beautiful. Mary was the easy going one; long suffering but patient, tolerant and reflective. Summer came all too soon. Yet more flowers bloomed to enrich the landscape. Yet more birds flew. Yet......Yet...... Yet the storm came too. And with the storms of nature came the storms of youth, pretty youth, pale youth, sparkling youth. First, the violence of the storm; now the violence of youth. Only Mary was calm; devoid of clouds. Then flowers died, and the birds left and there was a coolness in the air.

(Lx c/f to main area)
(enter Ginny)

GINNY Where's my dress?
ELLIE (ironing) Which dress?
GINNY The blue one.
ELLIE The long blue one, or the short blue one?
GINNY I'm wearing the long one.
(pause)
ELLIE In the drawer, I think.
GINNY Which drawer?
ELLIE Ginny, dear; you only have three drawers. One has your undies in, another your short skirts. God knows what's in the other one.

GINNY	You haven't been looking have you?
ELLIE	More than my life's worth. Anyway, your drawers are for your own private things. You've only your short skirts there because the rail's full in the wardrobe.
GINNY	Well there isn't much rail to speak of.
ELLIE	Your Dad an' me can manage with the amount you've got between us. I've never seen anyone else of your age with so many dresses. No wonder the rail's full.
GINNY	I am twenty!
ELLIE	What's that to do with it?
GINNY	Can't I have the clothes I want at twenty?
ELLIE	At twenty I had one skirt and two dresses.....
GINNY	That was years ago.
ELLIE	(continuing) One of those was for best. I was thirty before my rail was half full. The trouble with you these days......
GINNY	(sarcastically) These days is..
ELLIE	(ignoring Ginny)......is you're never satisfied with what you've got. First you want this, then that, then.....well you know what I'm going to say.
GINNY	Don't I just.
ELLIE	There's always something you have to buy.....
GINNY	So what? I'll please myself what I buy and when.
ELLIE	You've never got any money anyhow. Get yourself a job. Your father's been telling you that for I don't know how long.
GINNY	Well he can keep on telling me for all I care.
ELLIE	Now then, careful what you say.
GINNY	Well it is.
ELLIE	It's only your Dad's kindness that allows you to stay here; rent free as well. He is a good man you know.
GINNY	I'll pay if you've a problem with me staying here rent free.
ELLIE	What with? You've spent the last three years in and out of jobs. At the moment you're out, and not even making an effort to find one. How can you pay?
GINNY	I'll manage.
ELLIE	When?

GINNY	Soon.
ELLIE	How soon?
GINNY	Soon enough.
ELLIE	What does that mean? If you think.....
GINNY	Oh don't go on.
ELLIE	I wouldn't need to go on if you sorted yourself out. First it's the solicitors. Grandiose ideas I'm sure. That training lasted six weeks then it was straight on to the estate agent. That didn't last long either. Eight weeks holiday then the...
GINNY	It was not a holiday!
ELLIE	What was it then? You were at home with your feet up for eight weeks, that can hardly be called job searching. Then after that rest there was the old people's home, the dental surgery....oh I don't know where else...........
GINNY	So?
ELLIE	Only to be followed by a further period of rest and relaxation with no intention of getting a job.
GINNY	I found one though.
ELLIE	Call that a job. Part time at the local bar. You only took that 'cos Rick found it for you - on one of his outings.
GINNY	What do you mean?
ELLIE	You know very well what I mean. Anyway, you haven't got that now. You stupidly chucked that in.
GINNY	So what?
ELLIE	You can't stick at anything, Ginny. You have to realise that the world does not owe you a living.

(enter Mary)

MARY	Mum, what time will Dad be home tonight?
ELLIE	Why do you ask?
MARY	I was wondering...well....if he would well... you know it's Jo's party tonight?
ELLIE	Mmmm?
MARY	Well....I know that he's usually busy like but...
GINNY	For God's sake Mary, cough it up.

MARY	Could he collect me from Jo's sort of late?
ELLIE	What do you call late?
MARY	About two in the morning.
	Ah! Well who's going?
MARY	Well Jo will be there with Dave, and...
GINNY	All the other snotty friends she has.
MARY	Ginny! They're not...
GINNY	I expect you'll get an all expenses paid benefit because of your group of...
MARY	That's not fair!
GINNY	Why not?
MARY	Because....
GINNY	Of course it's fair.
MARY	Look Ginny, if you want to keep company with... well... layabouts, that's up to you. But don't criticise me for trying to....
GINNY	Suck up to the toffs
MARY	They're not toffs.
GINNY	What are they then?
MARY	They've just got decent jobs that's all.
GINNY	And I haven't, is that it?
MARY	Well...you haven't actually got one at all.
GINNY	I suppose that makes you feel good does it? All of your friends have got lots of money. I reckon they're doing what they do 'cos Daddy says so. They're in life for the money. They don't care for people and they can't stand on their own feet without Daddy says so. Rich? I tell you Mary, if they had half the guts that my Rick's got in standing up for what he believes in instead of the... 'Yes, sir....no sir.... three bags full sir...oh! and sir, is it possible to see you on Thursday about a small incentive allowance?' ...then they would be living, really living, instead of playing at dummies.
MARY	Ginny............
GINNY	Oh shit! Is that the time. See you dummy.
(exit Ginny)	

29

MARY	Oh Mum!
(pause)	
ELLIE	You'll have to ask your father you know.
MARY	I know.
ELLIE	He doesn't usually complain.
(pause)	
MARY	He's different Mum.
ELLIE	What do you mean?
MARY	He's changed.
ELLIE	The world's changing love.
MARY	No, I mean......well, something is different. He doesn't smile anymore.
ELLIE	He…
(pause)	
MARY	Mum?
ELLIE	Oh, nothing.
MARY	But mum...
ELLIE	Yes, love?
MARY	Please tell me.
ELLIE	There is nothing to tell. (slightly irritated)
(pause)	
MARY	Ginny's changed as well.
ELLIE	As I said. The world is changing.
MARY	Will I change Mum?
ELLIE	(pause) No dear. (smiling) Some people never change.

(Lx c/f to spot)

RICK (drinking) They done me. They bloody done me. No work, no pay. The bastards! I told them I didn't like their rules. I'll work. I'll work I said. I'll work hard. But your rules? Rules! Their rules! You can't do this. That's for others. 'Ole Jim'll do that. Wait for 'ole Jim? No chance! He takes bloody hours! I'll do it. Sod 'em. Sod their rules. I moved more in a morning than the others did in a day. The pay wasn't bad but, those bloody rules. You must wear that helmet, they said. Oh! Don't park the truck there. But it's quicker, I says. It's not safe, they says. You can't leave until it's done...can't leave it unfinished. It really got me. I worked harder than the lot of 'em but still I 'ad to finish the job I was doing. (pause) (change of mood) I looked forward to those evenings. Yeh!..the sounds, the smells, the booze, the.....yeh, that as well. It was what I had. it was my freedom. (pause) (returns to original mood) I could have… 'Look, if you don't like it then I'll piss off. Stuff those rules. Stuff your job! Stuff you!'

(B.O.)

(Lx fade up to main area)
(Geoff is reading. Ginny enters)

GINNY	Hi! Dad.
GEOFF	Hello love. Good day?
GINNY	Not bad. Lots of work though. Did you know that Phil passed his test yesterday?
GEOFF	Phil? Who's Phil?
GINNY	Phil, you know. Mr. Harris's eldest.
GEOFF	Oh! Of course. First time?
GINNY	Third.
GEOFF	Probably too confident. Lads his age always have too much confidence in themselves. If they passed first time they'd probably tear around the streets like no-one's business and cause an accident. It's best they don't pass first time.
GINNY	Oh! Dad. You can't generalise like that. Phil's a great lad. He's ever so careful.
GEOFF	I hope so.
GINNY	He is.
GEOFF	Perhaps. Perhaps not. We'll see.
GINNY	He wants me to go out with him and some friends.
GEOFF	When?
GINNY	Tonight.
GEOFF	Where to?
GINNY	Just out.

GEOFF	Where though?
GINNY	Nowhere in particular, I think.
GEOFF	How can you go 'just out' without going anywhere?
GINNY	Oh! Dad.
GEOFF	And who are these friends? Are they male or female? How old? And how are you getting there? Wherever 'there' is.
GINNY	Just friends, Dad. There's Becky, she's a female. And there's Rick, he's a male. And, of course, there's Phil. He's male too. They're all seventeen. Actually Rick's eighteen tomorrow. He'll probably have a party. By car and Phil's driving of course. It's his Dad's car, he says he can drive it if he pays for the petrol. Of course, it'll be Rick that actually pays for the petrol as he's the only one who works. And I'm sixteen, seventeen next month, female. I'll sit in the back with Rick. He's nice! (pause) You might not like his jacket, it's leather, but he's nice.
GEOFF	Now just wait a minute. You've got some friends. You're going out with your friends. But you're going nowhere in particular in a car driven by someone I vaguely know, who passed his test only yesterday, and you expect me to give you my blessing. Well I'm sorry love but that won't do. I'm not having you driving around the streets, I suppose for half the night, in a car with a young inexperienced driver. Can't you imagine how worried your mother and I might be, not knowing where you are, when you are going to return, if you are going to return. Just think of us. I'm sorry, love, but no.

(Lx fade to b/o over the next few lines)

GINNY	But, Dad, he drives well.
GEOFF	I said no.
GINNY	Why not, dad?
GEOFF	Shall we just call it responsible parenting?
GINNY	I am sixteen.
GEOFF	Ginny...
GINNY	Thats unreasonable, Dad.
GEOFF	Let me decide that.

GINNY   But, Dad.......

(Lx fade up to spot) (music in the background)
RICK   (drunk) Come on lads! Enjoys yourselves. There's plenty more where that came from. Drain your glasses and fill 'em up. (poshly) Bottoms up! What ho! (as normal) Hey, girls! Have another one, or two. Have six. You'll feel better. You know what I mean? Thats better. Soon be time to enjoy yourselves. Get my meaning. Yes, that's right. Drink up. Show the world you don't care a damn. Stuff the lot of them. Stuff the lot of them!

(Lx c/f to main area)
MARY   Ginny?
GINNY   What?
MARY   Where did you go last night?
GINNY   What's it to you?
MARY   I only asked.
GINNY   Well don't.
MARY   Ginny?
(pause)
GINNY   If you must know I was out with Rick.
MARY   I guessed that much.
GINNY   Well you don't really want a description of my activities do you?
MARY   I only asked.
MARY   (pause) Ginny?
(pause)
MARY   Ginny?
GINNY   What now?
(pause)
GINNY   Well?
MARY   Nothing.
(Lx fade to B.O.)

33

(Lx fade up main area)

RICK	So you got the job then?
GINNY	Yeh! Old Mr. Perkins seems all right. A bit straight though.
RICK	Tell me more!
GINNY	(pause) Is your job going all right?
RICK	Suppose.
GINNY	What's that meant to mean?
RICK	You know me, Gin. I like a bit of freedom.. (with a swagger)
GINNY	And?
RICK	Well I suppose I don't get it. Not enough like.
GINNY	How's that?
RICK	Oh, I dunno.
GINNY	You'll stick to it though?
RICK	Of course.
GINNY	Promise?
RICK	Well...
GINNY	Promise, Rick?
RICK	Gin....
GINNY	Promise?
RICK	Yeah!
GINNY	Thanks, Rick.
RICK	**Yeah well....**

(pause)

RICK	Gin?
GINNY	Yes.
RICK	(pause) Hey! You're a great girl Gin. Come here. (Ginny moves to Rick. They embrace)

GINNY Oh, Rick!

RICK   A great girl!

(Rick spins around holding Ginny)

GINN   Oh!!!!

(they fall laughing onto a soft chair)

RICK }	Ha..Ha..Ha..
GINNY}	Ha..Ha..Ha..

(they kiss and there is a freeze)

(Lx c/f to red for a few seconds and then c/f to normal lighting)
(they unfreeze and Rick rises)

RICK	Do you fancy a drink?
GINNY	You've been drinking already.
RICK	Just a bit.
GINNY	You shouldn't drink too much you know.
RICK	What's it to you?
GINNY	I care about you.
RICK	Why should that stop me drinking too much?
GINNY	Because I don't want to lose you.
RICK	You aren't going to lose me kid.
GINNY	To drink, I mean.
RICK	Do you think I'd leave you then?
GINNY	It's not that it's...
RICK	O.K., kid. I do understand. Really, I do.
GINNY	Sure?
RICK	Of course.
GINNY	All right, I believe you.
RICK	That's settled then. Do you want a drink now?
GINNY	Yeah. Yeah, I will.
RICK	Great. (pours a couple of drinks)
GINNY	(pause) I love you.
RICK	(handing drink to Ginny) Yeah, well!
GINNY	Seriously, Rick.
RICK	What do yer mean, kid?
GINNY	(grabbing Rick) I mean that I love you.

(Rick pulls away)

RICK	Oh don't put the pressure on kid.
GINNY	There's no pressure.
RICK	That's not how it feels.
GINNY	(putting drink on table) There's no pressure, Rick.

(pause)

GINNY	Look at me.
RICK	Mmmm?
GINNY	(pause) Look at me, Rick.

RICK	I can't, Gin.
GINNY	Rick?
RICK	You're good to me, Girl.
GINNY	And you're good to me.
RICK	But...
GINNY	But what?
RICK	It;s great being with you but...
GINNY	But what...?
RICK	I can't tell you.
GINNY	You're not usually slow at speaking your mind.
RICK	(angrily) I can't tell you.
GINNY	(pause) Is there someone else?
RICK	It's not like that.
GINNY	What is it like?
RICK	Ginny!
GINNY	(pause) I'm sorry, Rick.
RICK	Yeah!
GINNY	(pause) I think I'll have that drink now.
RICK	Yeah. (looks at his own glass) Me too.

(they drink for a while and then..)
(Lx c/f to spot)
(Rick walks into spot alone)

RICK   (miming handing glass to bar attendant) Another Scotch, mate. ...double... Cheers.... Cold? Yeah, it is...

(pause)
(Rick drinks up)

RICK   Same again, chief... Is..er..she...? Yeh? O.K!

(Rick mimes getting his glass refilled and then drinks it all)

RICK   (pause) Here you are, mate. One hour? Right!

(Rick mimes handing over money to the bar attendant and then walks slowly out of the spot and exits)

(Lx c/f to main area)
(enter Geoff)

GEOFF   Did the postman come?

ELLIE	Hello love. Only one. (points to the letter on the table)
GEOFF	What's it this time?
ELLIE	It's addressed to you....
GEOFF	Sorry!
ELLIE	...but I think it may be a bill.
GEOFF	Why is every other letter a bill?
ELLIE	It just seems that way. I don't suppose for a minute we have more bills than next door.
GEOFF	They're so bloody depressing.
ELLIE	I suppose we're only paying for what we've had.
GEOFF	Sometimes like they arrive every day though.
ELLIE	Time does pass quickly. (pause) Still, you must enjoy life and not worry about them. We can afford to pay them at least.
GEOFF	You're right of course. It's just that I am not really feeling right. I suppose that I am thinking about...
ELLIE	Ginny?
GEOFF	Yes. I feel that all I had wanted for her is no longer possible.
ELLIE	Geoff! Please.
GEOFF	Sorry.
ELLIE	Never mind, love.
GEOFF	It's just that there seems to be no calm between the storms.
ELLIE	I understand, love. Really, I do.
(pause)	
ELLIE	Are you in tonight?
GEOFF	I've finished for the week, thank God. I shall be pleased to get my feet up for a while.
ELLIE	Only Mary......
GEOFF	Wants a lift somewhere?
ELLIE	She's worried about asking you. It's the time see.
GEOFF	Late?
ELLIE	Very.
GEOFF	Where?
ELLIE	Jo's. There's a party.
GEOFF	I won't be able to sleep anyway.
ELLIE	She will appreciate it.

GEOFF   I know. I know.
(pause)
ELLIE   Dinner's nearly ready.
GEOFF   Oh, OK Thank you. You're good to me.
ELLIE   You're good to me.
(they embrace)
(exit Ellie)
(Geoff opens the letter)
(enter Mary)
MARY   Oh, Dad! You're home then?
GEOFF   Yes love.
MARY   Has Mum spoken to you?
GEOFF   Yes, love.
MARY   Will it be all right then?
GEOFF   (reading letter) Mm? What?
MARY   Tonight?
GEOFF   What about tonight.
MARY   Mum has spoken to you hasn't she?
GEOFF   Yes.
MARY   Well?
GEOFF   Oh that! Sorry, love. I was thinking. (pause) Yes, thats fine.
MARY   Thanks. Thanks a lot, Dad.
(Mary kisses Geoff and goes towards the exit)
MARY   Oh Dad?
GEOFF   Yes?
MARY   Nothing.
GEOFF   (pause) (to himself) Nothing!
MARY   Dad?
GEOFF   (realising that Mary has heard) Oh never mind.
MARY   I know something's wrong.
GEOFF   What do you mean?
MARY   Dad, look at me. I know something is wrong.
GEOFF   (pause) Yes. Something's wrong.
MARY   Is it Ginny?
GEOFF   It might be me

MARY	How can it be you? You understand people. You work with people, many people, complex people. Ginny is no more complex a person than you deal with every day.
GEOFF	She is my daughter.
MARY	That doesn't mean that she any more difficult to deal with than anyone else.
GEOFF	Why is that?
MARY	It is just a question of understanding.
GEOFF	(pensively) No. Family is different.
MARY	Families are just people too, Dad.
GEOFF	But just being people does not make them the same to deal with. And families are... Oh, I don't know.
MARY	(pause) Dad?
GEOFF	Yes?
MARY	You do know. You know how to deal with people. You know how to deal with Mum, me. I am sure that it is within you to deal with Ginny as well.
GEOFF	Yes, but I don't understand her. At least I do understand Mum.
MARY	You will. Think about it. I am sure that you will.
GEOFF	Do you?
MARY	Of course.
GEOFF	But will Ginny understand me?
MARY	Maybe. (smiles) Maybe.

(Lx c/f to spot)

ELLIE	Geoff's a good man, a kind man, a loving man. Ginny? ... well... she loved once. She was always independent, passionate, quick tempered but... not this. It didn't just happen. Not like that. They say time mends all. But, time it also destroys. Oh, it destroys. It leaves a wreck of families if their fragility permits. But why? It was almost three years ago, no...four. Geoff was never strict, not really, not like (pause) they used to be. Huh! Who's they? But he did love, he did care, he did...care. 'Be back by twelve', don't be late. 'Sure

'No, all right then but....take care.' She returned at three. She stank. Smoke... drink. 'So bloody what?' That hurt him. I could tell it hurt. It would have been forgiven... once. But once is not always. Four years is forever. It got much worse after that. No-one knew if she was going to return even... she always did. But when she returned she wasn't Ginny; pretty, pale, sparkling Ginny. She was stinking, drinking, unthinking Ginny. There were no thanks, no reasons, no love. I was the fool. I still did things for her, without thanks, but never questioned her way of life. I wanted to. Oh yes, I wanted to. There were arguments, many arguments, but I was not bitter. It's her life. I could not (pause) would not control that. Geoff hurt...more than anything to see his pretty, pale, sparkling Ginny... He felt rejected. He felt isolated. It was he who felt bitter, depressed and very hurt. He was changing.

(Lx c/f to main area)

RICK	Your old man been sticking his nose in again?
GINNY	He dare'nt. I've told him.
RICK	That's the spirit, my girl. Pay 'em back. Stick up for...
GINNY	Rick. That's enough.
RICK	Why? You're not going soft are you?
GINNY	Look, I've told you. That's enough.
RICK	(pause) Gin?
GINNY	Mmmm?
RICK	Can yer lend us a tenner?
GINNY	What for?
RICK	Does it matter?
GINNY	You're not usually that short.
RICK	Well I am and thats it!
GINNY	It's you that pulls in the money, not me.
RICK	(pause) Can you?
GINNY	I've told you.
RICK	But...
GINNY	(firmly) I've told you.
RICK	Yeh, well!

GINNY	(pause) You've finished early today.
RICK	(pause, ignoring Ginny) You working tonight?
GINNY	Eight onwards.
RICK	Till when?
GINNY	Two.
RICK	Or three....
GINNY	So?
RICK	I hardly see you.
GINNY	You got me the job. It is only four nights......
RICK	It doesn't pay?
GINNY	...But I need the money. I've got to pay rent.
RICK	At your 'ole man's?
GINNY	Why not?
RICK	He's a.....
GINNY	Rick!.
RICK	(pause) We should get somewhere.
GINNY	How?
RICK	Money of course!
GINNY	You and me both don't earn earn enough to take a slum.
RICK	There's a squat.....
GINNY	I'm not interested.
RICK	Why not?
GINNY	I've got a bit of pride left.
RICK	What good's that without freedom?
GINNY	I've learnt a lot from you, Rick. I've learnt my independence. I've learnt to stand up for myself. I've learnt how not to get pushed to the bottom of the pile. I'd had enough of that. (aside) Yes, Mary, love. Of course! Do you want to...? Ginny won't mind. (angrily) Ginny will mind. Ginny always minds. Ginny is sick of minding. Sick! (calmly) God knows it's not your fault, Mary. I know we're different. So very different. But you always won the game... the game you never played. Daddy and Mummy played the game for you. You unseated the king and took the throne. You just watched as the world passed

by. (to Rick) The job in the bar....it's my only freedom. You helped me with that. Because you're ndependent, I want to be independent. You got that job for me. But how? (puzzled) That was never your bar. It's filled with fat, red faced men with even fatter pockets. Girls who would sooner take your money than talk to you… and even sooner...

(pause...Ginny stares at Rick)

RICK	We did a deal.
GINNY	You knew didn't you?
RICK	There's good pay...eventually.
GINNY	Bastard.
RICK	Come on girl. I did it for us.
GINNY	We're through!
RICK	But Ginny...
GINNY	You heard.
RICK	But I need you. You can't go. I'm not independent, not really. Once, yeh well!… once. But now? No, not now. I need you. I told 'em though. They weren't pushing me around. Them and their rules. Bloody rules. But I showed 'em. I told them to stuff their job..
GINNY	You stupid fool!

(exit Ginny)

RICK	Ginny? Wait!

(enter Ellie)

ELLIE	(softly) Rick? (Rick cannot hear Ellie's words. He freezes and continues to look after Ginny) Rick? She is learning fast. She knows you now. Knows what you are. You are no more. She's in the distance now… fading you know. Fading… fading….

(Ellie's voice fades)

(Lx c/f to spot)

GINNY	It's Autumn now. Spring was such a long time ago - it seems like a hundred years. Summer was love. He swept me from the clutches of the dragon breathing fire. He swept me to the wonderful world of freedom, of independence… of love. Oh

what love! There were many storms that summer but love reigned over them all. The storms were a disease, a crippling disease slowly encroaching on the freedom of youth, my youth. Love was the drug. The wonder drug that held the storms at bay and, for a time, appeared to cure. But that cure did not last. The storms continued but I could no longer take such weather. The love was fading and the storms took over all. He mocked me and my new found freedom. But I mocked him. I rejected him. It took all of me, sapping every last drop of what I had. I am weak now, very weak, and the storms must surely end. They must surely end.

(Lx c/f to main area)
MARY   I know now, Mum
ELLIE   Ginny....?
MARY   And Dad.
(pause)
ELLIE   Good.
MARY   Will it change?
ELLIE   You can make it change.
MARY   But..
ELLIE   You can make it happen.
MARY   How?
ELLIE   Just think a while.
(exits)

(Fx a storm is heard)
MARY   Oh, Ginny! Dear, Ginny! Can't you hear him call? The storm is loud. He's looking for you. He's reaching you. Can't you hear him? Nearly there now. Yes! Now! He's touching you. Can't you hear him still?
(Fx storm ceases)
(Rick enters) (Mary's responses are almost ethereal)
RICK   Where is she then?
MARY   Who?

RICK	You know who.
MARY	You've lost her.
RICK	What do you mean, 'lost her'?
MARY	The wind has dropped.
RICK	What wind?
MARY	The storm has stopped.
RICK	What do you mean?
MARY	It's getting lighter.
RICK	You're mad!
MARY	It is not me. No, not me.
RICK	(pause) Got a light....?
MARY	(pauses then looks towards the window) The Sun is shining.....
RICK	No?
MARY	Appearing from behind the clouds. What clouds? There are no clouds. The clouds have gone. (smiles)
RICK	I'm off.
MARY	(breathes in the air as she gazes around) It's Spring again.

(exit Rick)

(Mary walks downstage)

(Lx c/f to spot)

MARY   I can hear birds now. They call so sweetly. The sun shines brightly now. There is no haze. The leaves hang from once barren trunks and chatter merrily in the wind. They're playing games. Yes, I see them now, the birds, they're playing games ...singing games, dancing games, courting games... (laughs). It is a happy time… a sad time. Life is so short yet, everything is happy. It is the same every year. The flowers bloom, their colours… oh such bright colours... cheer the very soul. The trees start pale and deepen as the days grow long. The birds are out building their nests. No! It is a happy time. A time for smiling. (smiles) A time worth waiting for. A time when all the earth eagerly waits for its chance to flourish. The return of Spring.

(Lx c/f to main area)

GEOFF	(looking through an imaginary window) It's raining again. How depressing.
GINNY	(speaking to Geoff, but he does not really hear her - he does not even realise her presence) The clouds are very dark.
GEOFF	Very dark clouds.

(Fx a distant rumble of thunder is heard)

GINNY	(pointing) There is a storm over there.
GEOFF	Listen, you can just hear the thunder in the distance.
GINNY	It is passing.
GEOFF	No lightning though.
GINNY	The church tower was struck earlier today.
GEOFF	Why no lightning?
GINNY	No damage.
GEOFF	I wonder why.
GINNY	No-one hurt.
GEOFF	Well, no-one hurt.
GINNY	No-one.
GEOFF	No families have suffered.
GINN	(pause) It is passing.
GEOFF	There's a breeze getting up.
GINNY	The clouds are moving faster.
GEOFF	(starting to be aware of a conversation) Perhaps the storm will pass.
GINNY	The storm!
GEOFF	Perhaps it will pass.
GINNY	And the day?
GEOFF	It will get better I am sure.
GINNY	I am sure too.

(pause)

GEOFF	There's just a hint of sunlight coming from behind the clouds.
GINNY	Yes, look! The storm is clearing.
GEOFF	Quite quickly too.
GINNY	It has been a long time.
GEOFF	A very long time.
GINNY	(pause) And now...

(together)
GINNY }The storm has passed.
GEOFF }The storm has passed.
(Ginny puts her hand on Geoff's shoulder. Geoff turns slowly and sees Ginny)
GEOFF   The storm has passed.
GINNY   Yes.
GEOFF   Will it return?
GINNY   No.
GEOFF   Never?
GINNY   Never!
GEOFF   Thank you.
GINNY   Oh! Dad, I'm sorry. I'm so very sorry.
GEOFF   Thank you (they embrace)

THE END

The Forest Path

a drama

Characters

Pauline	a patient
Rachel	a patient
Ralph	a care worker
Alf	an old patient
David	a young patient
Ruth	a care worker
Dinah	a young woman server

Other characters as required.

Pauline lives in a world of complete imagination. She is cared for by Ruth who talks to her but Pauline rarely makes sense in what she says. She cannot exist outside of the home in which she has been accepted. Much that passes in this play is in her mind. Some of the speeches and conversations are spoken by the actors in their rôles but are imagined by Pauline.

(Lx spot on area around Pauline)

(Pauline sits on a small rocky outcrop overlooking a winding forest path. She talks to herself)

PAULINE   I sit and gaze over the winding path through the forest. The sun is low in the sky and the birds sweetly chatter. The dew is still heavy on the grass. I am alone. I am waiting for my friend. My friend will come. It is a long way. It is a long way from the town, It is a long way up the hill. It is a long way through the forest. It is a long way along the winding path. It is a long way. It is...(pause) ...a long way. A kestrel hangs in the sky above the grassy outcrop at the forest edge. He waits patiently. (pause) He still waits patiently. He waits as I wait. He waits patiently for his prey to show itself. I wait patiently for my friend. His prey will come. My friend will come. My friend will come along the forest path. From the town my friend will come. Along the path. Up the hill. Along the path. Through the forest. Along the path, the winding path; emerging from the forest edge and greeting me and I am waiting here. I am waiting for my friend. My friend will come; from the town; up the hill; along the path; through the forest; to greet me here where I am waiting. Waiting for my friend. Just like the kestrel. The kestrel waits. The kestrel waits above the grassy outcrop. Hanging in the sky above the forest edge. Waiting. Waiting. Waiting. (pause) The sun is higher now. It lifts its smiling face above the shorter scrub which bounds the forest edge. The rustling tops of scrubby growth glisten golden in the rising sun. The smiling sun. It is early, and I am waiting. Waiting for my friend. Waiting for my friend to come along the winding path through the forest. My friend will come. But it is a long way. A long way from the town. It is a long way up the hill. It is a long way through the forest. It is a long way along the winding path. It is... (pause) ...a long way.(pause) Why are they rustling? Why? The tops of the scrubby golden growth. Why should they rustle? Why must they rustle? (smiles) I know. (pause) It must be the wind.

(Lx c/f to another spot)

RACHEL   I am Pauline's friend. I am going to see Pauline. I am walking. The sun is low in the sky and the birds sweetly chatter. The dew is still heavy on the grass. I am alone I am walking to my friend. My friend will be there. I am … walking. It is a long way. It is a long way from the town. It is a long way up the hill. It is a long way through the forest. It is a long way along the winding path. It is a long way. A kestrel hangs in the sky above the grassy outcrop at the forest edge. He waits patiently. (pause) He still waits patiently. He waits as I walk. He waits patiently for his prey to show itself. I am walking patiently to my friend. His prey will come. My friend will wait for me. My friend will wait at the end of the forest path. I am walking from the town to meet my friend. My friend will wait and I will come along the path. Up the hill. Along the path. Through the forest. Along the path, the winding path; emerging from the forest edge and greeting her. I am walking. I am walking to my friend. My friend will wait while I am walking from the town; up the hill; along the path; through the forest; to greet her there where she is waiting. Waiting for me; her friend. Just like the kestrel. The kestrel waits. The kestrel waits above the grassy outcrop. Hanging in the sky above the forest edge. Waiting. Waiting. Waiting. (pause) The sun is higher now. It lifts its smiling face above the shorter scrub which bounds the forest edge. The rustling tops of scrubby growth glisten golden in the rising sun. The smiling sun. It is early, and I am walking. Walking to my friend. Walking to my friend along the winding path through the forest. My friend will wait. But it is a long way. A long way from the town. It is a long way up the hill. It is a long way through the forest. It is a long way along the winding path. It is..(pause) …a long way. (pause) Why are they rustling? Why? The tops of the scrubby golden growth. Why should they rustle? Why must they rustle? (smiles) I know. (pause) It must be the wind.

(Lx c/f to another spot where Ralph is resting)

RALPH	Hello! I am Ralph. I live here. I have lived here a long time. Do you live here.. (quickly) ..no! Of course you don't. It is nice here. It is a nice town. And all around the town there are fields. With walls. Or fences. With gates. And hills. And trees. And paths. And a forest. Ha! Ha! People walk along the paths. And in the town. There are lots of paths across the hills. And in the town. And by the walls and fences. And through the gates. And into the forest. (pause) It's dark in there. The forest. But there are paths. A path. A long path. A windy path. A long windy path. Everyone knows it. Everyone knows it as the forest path. The long windy path through the forest. Everyone does. (pause) There is a grassy outcrop at the forest edge. Things live there. Birds. A kestrel. It is so beautiful. You can see it often. Hanging in the sky. Near the path. At the forest edge. There is a seat there. A large seat. A bench. (pause) You can sit there. On the bench. It is high. There is a view. A good view. A good view over the valley. Over the forest. Over the path. The winding path. The winding path through the forest. The long winding path through the forest. I expect it is there now. Not the bench. The kestrel. Hanging in the sky. Above the grassy outcrop near the forest edge. Hanging. Waiting. Waiting for its prey. (pause) Of course, the bench is there too. High above the valley. Overlooking the forest. And the forest path. And the kestrel. Hanging. Waiting. Waiting for its prey. Just like the bench. I work here too. I have for a long time. Not in the town. But near the town. In a large mansion overlooking the valley. Not near the bench. The other side. But you can see the bench from the mansion. And the forest. And the path. And the kestrel. When it is there. Hanging. Waiting. I love that valley.

(Lx c/f to another spot)

ALF	I am old now. Eighty nine. Lived here ever since I was a lad. Very small. Very young. Now I am very old. I'm Alf. They call me Alfie. All of 'em call me Alfie. I don't know why. I'm just Alf.

They won't listen. Not to me. There are too many of them. Too many to listen. To me. When you gets old there isn't much you can do. Every day. It comes often. Every day. Sometimes I walk. Sometimes I just sit. Walk. Sit. Walk. Sit. Today I am sitting. Just sitting. I am looking across the gardens. All flowers. Nice flowers. Smell nice. Very nice. (pause) I can't see the flowers. I am too old. My eyes. My eyes you see. They're old too. They can't see the flowers. Not well. But the flowers are there. They're beautiful. Smell nice. I am old but I can still smell. Smell the flowers. That's how I know. How I know that the gardens are nice. The smell. I am old but I still know. There is much I know although I am old. Much. (pause) They don't believe me of course. They think because you're old you don't know. But you do. Everything. I can hear. I listen. I listen to everything that goes on. I can't see but I listen and I can hear. And smell. It tells you a lot. Everything. I can smell the lilacs and the roses, the lavender and the... the... (pause) Someone is coming. I can't see them but I can smell them. In the wind. In the air. And hear them move. However lightly they step. I know they are coming. I know. I just know. it's Ralph.

(Ralph enters)

RALPH	Hello Alfie.
ALF	Hello Ralphie! (smiles)
RALPH	The morning's bright...
ALF	A wonderful sight.
RALPH	And the sky is blue...
ALF	How are you?
RALPH	It is hot.
ALF	I am not.
RALPH	I'm fine, and you?
ALF	Can't see the blue...
RALPH	It smells so clean.
ALF	Better than I have been.
RALPH	The mist has cleared.

ALF	Lucky you!
RALPH	And the dew...
ALF	Just as I feared...
RALPH	Is still heavy on the grass and the rest...
ALF	Just as I thought. Mind my chest.
RALPH	...of the valley floor.
ALF	Keep warm! Or you'll be poorly.
RALPH	How long are you sitting here, Alfie? All day.
ALF	Makes no difference. Whatever I say.
RALPH	You'll sit 'till two, that's my hunch.
ALF	They'll come and get me in for lunch.
RALPH	You're right of course.
ALF	Of course!
RALPH	As always.
ALF	Always.
RALPH	Yes... (pause) ...well! (looks around at the weather)
ALF	Well?
RALPH	No worse.
ALF	Than what?
RALPH	Yesterday.
(pause)	
ALF	What's the time?
RALPH	Nine.
ALF	Sure?
RALPH	I heard the clock strike.
ALF	How many?
RALPH	Four.
(pause)	
ALF	It's nine then.
RALPH	Yes.
(pause)	
RALPH	It's hot!
ALF	I'm not.
RALPH	Alfie!...
ALF	Alf.

(pause)

RALPH	Did you hear the kestrel?
ALF	No.
RALPH	Above the grassy outcrop...
ALF	No.
RALPH	At the forest edge...
ALF	No.
RALPH	Hanging...
ALF	You can't hear the hanging.
RALPH	Floating...
ALF	You can't hear the floating.
RALPH	You can see the kestrel hanging there...
ALF	I can't.
RALPH	When it dives...
ALF	No!
RALPH	When it picks up its prey...
ALF	I can hear it then.
RALPH	It is a wonderful sight...
ALF	It's not!
RALPH	And sound...
ALF	Yes.
RALPH	Diving into the grassy outcrop at the forest edge...
ALF	The smell is beautiful.
RALPH	You can smell the kestrel?
ALF	The flowers.
RALPH	There are no flowers there.
ALF	The garden.
RALPH	The garden?
ALF	Yes.

(Lx c/f to another spot)

PAULINE It must be nine. The clock has struck. The clock in the town. On the church tower. It has struck four, so it must be nine. It always strikes four at nine o'clock. It always does. I expect she's coming along the path now. It takes a time. A long time.

It's a long path. Through the forest. The sun is bright now, very bright. There is no dew on the grass. There is no kestrel. The kestrel is not waiting any more. Not hanging. Not waiting for its prey. It has eaten now. It has had its breakfast. Just like me. I have eaten my breakfast. I am not hungry. Not any more. But I am still waiting here for my friend. The kestrel is not hungry. It has eaten. It is not waiting any more. Not like me. I am still waiting for my friend. Rachel. She will be here by lunchtime. I will wait for her.

(Lx c/f to another spot)

RACHEL   It's getting warmer now. The sun is bright in the sky. I am still walking to meet a friend. Pauline. I will meet her at lunchtime. It is a long walk. It is not lunchtime now. I am not hungry. It is still early. I have just heard the clock on the church tower strike four. It must be nine o'clock. It always strikes four at nine o'clock. Always. The dew has gone from the grass. The kestrel has gone from the sky. It is not there any more. Not hanging. Not waiting. Not hungry. Like me.

(Lx c/f to another spot)
(There are two people sitting opposite sides of a small table playing draughts. Dinah and David play slowly and deliberately. This lasts for about a minute. Dinah groans and David gets excited and waves his arms around in celebration)

(Lx c/f to another spot)
RUTH   It is warmer now, David. Warmer now. It was damp earlier. Much earlier. The dew has cleared now. From the grass. It is past nine now. The clock has struck.
DAVID   Four?
RUTH   Four.
DAVID   I wonder why.
RUTH   Why...?
DAVID   Why it strikes four.

RUTH	Because it is nine o'clock.
DAVID	But four?
RUTH	The church clock always strikes four at nine o'clock.
DAVID	Why?
RUTH	There are some things that just happen. No-one knows why. They just happen. Just like the church clock. Striking four. At nine. Maybe it is very old and has not been looked after. No-one knows. It just happens. Some things just happen.
DAVID	Some things just happen.
RUTH	Yes.
DAVID	Why are we here? (gazes upwards)
RUTH	Why...?
DAVID	Why? Here?
RUTH	We just are....
DAVID	We just are.
RUTH	Yes.

(Lx c/f to another spot)
(Ralph and Dinah enter from different directions)

RALPH	Is it ready?
DINAH	Ready?
RALPH	Dinner?
DINAH	Dinner?
RALPH	Yes, dinner?
DINAH	Oh!
RALPH	Well?
DINAH	No.
RALPH	Oh!

(pause)

DINAH	Soon.
RALPH	What?
DINAH	Soon.
RALPH	Soon what?
DINAH	Dinner.
RALPH	Oh, dinner.

DINAH	Yes.
RALPH	Good.
DINAH	Yes, good.

(pause)

DINAH	Yes.
RALPH	That will be nice.
DINAH	Nice. Yes.
RALPH	Very nice.
DINAH	Very nice.

(Lx c/f to another spot)

ALF   I can smell it now. It's a fair distance away but I can still smell it. When you get old you can't walk. When you get old you can't see. But you can still think. (pause) ....and smell. Eighty nine! Eighty nine years I've been. Eighty nine. (pause) I like to sit here watching, listening... (pause) ... smelling. I can't see very much. My eyes you see. But I can hear. I can smell. I can smell now. Smell what? Lunch! I can smell it for miles. When I can smell it I know that lunch is near. Soon they will come and get me. Get me for lunch. I know. (pause) Those flowers are beautiful. The colours are like a rainbow .. vibrant. The dew of the morning glistens on the petals and paints a never to be forgotten picture. (pause) A memory. (pause) I can't see them of course. But I can smell them. Smell the fragrance. Smell the colours. Smell the dew. Smell the vibrance. Smell the glistening. They're coming now. I can hear them. It's two o'clock and the clock is about to strike. (the clock strikes nine) Ah yes! Nine! It is two o'clock.

(A young man in a white coat enters, helps Alf into a wheelchair and pushes him off stage)

(Lx c/f to another spot)

RALPH	There is a problem.
RUTH	I know.
RALPH	She is worse.

RUTH	Much worse?
RALPH	Much.
RUTH	And him?
RALPH	Fairly stable.
RUTH	Good.
RALPH	As good as can be expected.
RUTH	Then that is good.
RALPH	Yes. I suppose you're right.

(pause)

RUTH	She wanted to go into the garden today.
RALPH	Today?
RUTH	Yes, today.
RALPH	Did she?
RUTH	Yes.
RALPH	Why?
RUTH	She wanted to listen to the clock. To the birds. To the trees. To the air.
RALPH	It will help her.
RUTH	Yes I know.
RALPH	She wanted to walk.
RUTH	Walk?
RALPH	Yes.
RUTH	Where?
RALPH	Just walk.
RUTH	Just walk?
RALPH	Yes.

(pause)

RUTH	She must be careful.
RALPH	Of course.
RUTH	She likes to walk.
RALPH	Yes.
RUTH	She likes to walk a long way.
RALPH	A long way.
RUTH	Yes.

(pause)

RUTH	She must be careful.
RALPH	Of course.
RUTH	She likes to walk.
RALPH	Yes.
RUTH	She likes to walk a long way.
RALPH	A long way. (knowingly)
RUTH	Yes.
(pause)	
RALPH	She likes the forest?
RUTH	The forest. (nodding)
RALPH	And the path?
RUTH	The path. (nodding)
RALPH	Well?
(pause)	
RUTH	Yes.
(pause)	
RUTH	The path is long. It is a long walk. That is why she likes the path. Do you see?
RALPH	Of course.
RUTH	But she must be careful.
RALPH	Yes, of course.
RUTH	And him?
RALPH	Him?
RUTH	Him. You know.
RALPH	He sat in the garden all of the morning. Just sat. Alone.
RUTH	Except for the birds.
RALPH	And the flowers.
RUTH	And the kestrel.
RALPH	The kestrel.
RUTH	Yes.
(pause)	
RALPH	He is well enough.
RUTH	Of course... (pause) ...of course.
RALPH	It is wonderful how he knows...
RUTH	Knows?

RALPH	....everything. Yes, everything.
RUTH	Yes.
RALPH	He cannot see. Not far.
RUTH	No.
RALPH	But he can hear......
RUTH	And smell....
RALPH	Yes. And smell.
RUTH	Everything.
RALPH	Yes, everything.
RUTH	Everything.

(Lx c/f to another spot)
(Rachel, Alfie, Dinah, David and others are sitting at a table finishing their meal)

RUTH	Well now, that was nice wasn't it?
ALL	Yes. (general groans of approval)
RUTH	The dinner.
ALF	It's not dinner.
DAVID	Not dinner.
ALF	Not dinner.
ALL	Not dinner. Not dinner. Not dinner...
RUTH	All right! All right! Why the fuss?
ALF	Not dinner. Lunch.
DAVID	Lunch.
ALL	(except Ruth) Lunch. Lunch. Lunch...
RUTH	All right! All right! Lunch for goodness sake! What does it matter? What does it matter?
ALF	It matters. Of course it matters. Otherwise we wouldn't know the time of day. Not if it's dinner. Lunch is at two.
DAVID	Two.
ALF	Dinner is at seven.
DAVID	Seven.
ALF	If it's dinner then it's seven, but it's two.
DAVID	Seven, but it's two.

ALF	You know it's two. You can tell it's two.
DAVID	Tell.
ALF	The clock.
DAVID	Clock.
ALF	The clock's struck. So you know it's not seven.
DAVID	Not seven. (louder) Not seven. (louder still) Not seven...
RUTH	(shouting) Lunch it is. Not dinner. Do you all hear? Not dinner. It is lunch. All right?
ALL	Yes. (general groans of approval)
(pause)	
DAVID	Seven.
ALF	That's dinner.
DAVID	Se..se..seven.
ALF	I've said already.
DAVID	Seven is porridge.
ALF	It's not.
DAVID	(louder) It's porridge. It's porridge.
DINAH	(starting to cry) I can't make porridge.
ALF	You don't have porridge for dinner.
RUTH	He means breakfast Alfie. That's at seven.
ALF	I don't like porridge. I don't have it at seven.
RUTH	You've upset Dinah now.
DINAH	(crying) He doesn't like my porridge.
RUTH	Don't pay any attention, dear. He doesn't eat porridge anyway. We all like your porridge. Don't we?
ALL	(except Alf) Yes. (groans of approval)
RUTH	All of us.
ALL	(except Alf) Yes.
RUTH	There, Dinah. See? They all like your porridge.
ALF	Hmph!
RACHEL	I like your porridge, Dinah.
DINAH	(smiles) Mmm.
RACHEL	So does my friend.
DINAH	(still smiling) Mmm.
RACHEL	My friend, Pauline.

DINAH (smiling) Thank you Rachel. You're my friend, Rachel.
RACHEL   I'm your friend.
DINAH   And your friend.
RACHEL   My friend.
DINAH   Your friend is my friend.
RACHEL   My friend, Pauline?
DINAH   Yes.
RACHEL   She is your friend too?
DINAH   Yes.
RACHEL   You know my friend?
DINAH   Yes.
RACHEL   You know Pauline?
RUTH   That's enough, Rachel. Dinah is getting a little tired now. She must rest before she starts to get the dinner.
ALF   When's dinner, Dinah?
DAVID   (chanting) Dinner, Dinah! Dinner, Dinah! Dinner, Dinah!...
RUTH   David! Quiet! Come along, Dinah. You must rest now.
DINAH   Rest.
RUTH   Yes. That's right.
DINAH   Rest.
RUTH   (exiting with Dinah) Come along. There's a good girl.
(pause)
ALF   It'll be dinner soon. I want to go to the garden.
DAVID   Garden. Garden. (pause then slowly and quietly chants) Dinner, Dinah! Dinner, Dinah! Dinner, Dinah!...
(Lx c/f to another spot)
RALPH   Are they finished now?
RUTH   Finished?
RALPH   Lunch.
RUTH   Oh!
RALPH   Well?
RUTH   Yes.
RALPH   Good.
RUTH   I think so.
RALPH   What?

RUTH	Yes.
(pause)	
RALPH	Where is David?
RUTH	With the others.
RALPH	Having lunch?
RUTH	I've told you already.
RALPH	What?
RUTH	It's finished.
RALPH	Finished?
RUTH	Lunch.
RALPH	Oh, sorry! (pause) And David?
RUTH	No, after. In the room.
RALPH	Oh.
RUTH	He is playing.
RALPH	With the others.
RUTH	Yes.
RALPH	Good. He is better when he is not alone.
RUTH	Yes.
RALPH	Like...
RUTH	Yes.
RALPH	He is content.
RUTH	So are they all.
RALPH	Yes.
RUTH	Usually.
RALPH	Always.
RUTH	Usually.
(pause)	
RUTH	Dinah....
RALPH	Yes.
RUTH	..... is resting now.
RALPH	As always.
RUTH	Always?
RALPH	Always!
RUTH	Yes. (pause) They argued.
RALPH	As always?

RUTH	As always.
RALPH	Always.
RUTH	Yes.

(Lx c/f to another spot)

RACHEL	I walked a long way today. Miles. Along the path. The long path. The windy path. The long windy path through the forest. The trees are beautiful. The flowers are beautiful. The birds are beautiful. Beautiful. And at the end of the path at the edge of the forest (pause) there is the valley. The beautiful valley. The great big beautiful valley. There is a grassy outcrop at the edge of the forest. Sometimes there are birds there as well. Some times there is kestrel. Sometimes the kestrel is hanging. Waiting. Waiting for its prey. (pause) There is a seat there too. Near the grassy outcrop at the edge of the forest. There is always someone there. Sitting. Sitting on the seat at the edge of the forest. Waiting. (pause) Today it is my friend. Pauline. She was waiting for me. Waiting for me to walk along the forest path to meet her. (pause) We met. (pause) We talked. (pause) We talked for a long time. Today. (pause, then as she says the next lines she begins to rock gently to and fro faster and faster) I like Pauline. Pauline is nice. She is my friend. We talk. We talk a lot. I like talking. I like talking to Pauline. Pauline is my friend. My friend. My friend. (chants) Pauline. Friend. Pauline. Friend. Pauline. Friend. Pauline....

(Lx c/f to another spot)

ALF	(in a wheelchair) That was good. Lunch. It is always good. Lunch. It is always the same. Meat. Vegetables. Potatoes. Jelly. Very good. Same every day. Same meat. Same vegetables. Same jelly. Same time. Two o'clock. Two o'clock as always. Same smell. A wonderful smell. There's nothing to compare with the smell of lunch. Nothing. Nothing except the smell of the air. Fresh air. The fresh air from across the fields. From the garden. From across the valley. From across the forest. The fresh air bringing the smells of the flowers, of the hills, of the forest. Of the kestrel. The kestrel hanging above

the floor of the valley at the forest edge. Oh what wonderful smells they are. All of them. (pause) Here we are then. In the garden. It is beautiful here. It smells so nice. So fresh. The flowers are beautiful. They have many colours I cannot see. But I hear the sounds. The sounds of the flowers. I can touch the flowers. I can smell the flowers. I can taste the flowers in the air. (pause) Taste, touch, smell, hear. (pause) See. No! Not see. I cannot see the flowers. I can hear them. I can touch them. I can smell them. I can taste them in the air. But I cannot see them. No, not see. But I love them. Love them.

(Lx c/f to another spot)
(Dinah is seen lying down asleep)

(Lx c/f to another spot)
(David is seen weaving or knitting)

DAVID (finishing his work) There! It is done. It is done now. It is finished. It is finished now. All finished. I like it. I am happy with it. Very happy. It pleases me. It pleases me. I have done well. Very well. Well done, David. Well done. Ha! Ha! Ha! (pause then David pulls the woven item close to his cheek and caresses it lovingly) You're my friend. My best friend. I haven't got any friends at all except you. I like you. You make me very happy. Very, very happy. (pause) Friends always make me happy. I love my friends. All of them. But you're my very best friend. I love you.

(Lx c/f to another spot)
RACHEL   Hello, Dinah.
DINAH   Hello.
RACHEL   Have you seen her?
DINAH   Who?
RACHEL   My friend.
DINAH   Friend?
RACHEL   You know!
DINAH   (puzzled) Friend?

RACHEL	Pauline.
DINAH	Who?
RACHEL	Pauline.
DINAH	Pauline?
RACHEL	Yes.
DINAH	Friend.
RACHEL	Friend! Pauline.
DINAH	Pauline? Friend.
RACHEL	Yes.
DINAH	(slightly pausing) No.
RACHEL	But I met her today.
DINAH	No.
RACHEL	I did.
DINAH	Pauline?
RACHEL	I walked miles and miles and miles to meet her.
DINAH	Today?
RACHEL	Yes.
DINAH	Friend?
RACHEL	Yes.
DINAH	Pauline?
RACHEL	Yes.
DINAH	Today?
RACHEL	Yes.
DINAH	What time?
RACHEL	Today. Earlier.
DINAH	I cooked lunch.
RACHEL	Before.
DINAH	Before?
RACHEL	Before lunch.
DINAH	No. I cooked lunch.
RACHEL	All day?
DINAH	All morning. Before lunch.
RACHEL	So you didn't see her then?
DINAH	Friend?
RACHEL	Yes.

DINAH	No.
(pause)	
RACHEL	(sadly) Oh! (pause) What time is dinner?
DINAH	Later.
RACHEL	Later?
DINAH	Seven.
RACHEL	Seven.
DINAH	When the clock strikes.....
RACHEL	What?
DINAH	...two.
RACHEL	Strikes two.
DINAH	Yes.
RACHEL	Yes.
DINAH	You'll know it's dinner then.
RACHEL	Yes.
(pause)	
RACHEL	I like dinner.
(pause)	
RACHEL	What is dinner?
DINAH	Seven o'clock, dinner.
RACHEL	What is dinner?
DINAH	Soup.
RACHEL	Soup. I like soup.
DINAH	And bread.
RACHEL	I like soup.
DINAH	And salad.....
RACHEL	I like bread...
DINAH	...with eggs...
RACHEL	...and salad...
DINAH	...and chips.
RACHEL	...and eggs...
DINAH	That's all.
RACHEL	...and chips.
(Ruth enters)	
RUTH	Ah! There you are, Rachel. What are you doing here?

RACHEL	I like dinner.
RUTH	Dinner won't be long will it, Dinah?
RACHEL	I like soup.
DINAH	Not long.
RACHEL	It's nice.
RUTH	What's nice?
DINAH	Soup first...
RACHEL	Soup.
DINAH	...with bread.
RUTH	Oh! That is nice!
DINAH	Then salad with eggs...
RACHEL	}
RUTH	}(together) And chips!
DINAH	}

(They all laugh together as the lights fade)
(Lx c/f to another spot)

RALPH	All ready, David?
DAVID	David ready.
RALPH	Good. Shall we go then?
DAVID	Go?
RALPH	In to dinner.
DAVID	In to dinner?
RALPH	Yes. It's soup.
DAVID	Dinah?
RALPH	Yes that's right. Dinah cooks dinner.
DAVID	Dinah, dinner.
RALPH	Yes. Come along, David.
DAVID	Come along, David.
RALPH	Yes. That's right.
DAVID	David is coming for dinner.

(Lx c/f to another spot)
(Alf sits alone in his wheel chair. The church clock is heard to chime two)

ALF	Seven o'clock.

(pause)

ALF It's time for dinner. They'll take me away soon. Away from my thoughts. Away from the sights in my mind. Away from the smells. Away from the sounds of silence. But I shall remember them. Remember the sights. Remember the smells. Remember the sounds. Always.

(pause)

ALF Always.

(Ruth enters and pushes the wheel chair into the darkness)

(Lx c/f to another spot)

PAULINE The sun has set. The kestrel has gone. The valley smells sweet against the evening. The forest rustled in the twilight breeze. Rachel did not come. She walked but she did not come. Alf sat and gazed across the valley and then... and then he disappeared. Gone. Forever gone. The others never came. Not for me or with me or to me. Not ever. No-one. I am alone. I have always been alone. I will stay alone. Alone. Alone in my body. Alone in my mind. Alone in my mind? No! Not alone in my mind. My body is alone but I can share my mind. I can always share my mind. My thoughts are there to be shared with everyone. Everyone I want to be there.

(pause)

Alf is there. Grumpy old Alf. And Dinah. Dear, dear Dinah. Such a lovely sweet thing. And David. His mind is gone. And Ralph...

(Ruth enters)

RUTH Pauline? There you are. How have you been today. Tell me what you have been doing today.

PAULINE I have been sitting. Sitting alone. I have seen people. Lots of people. They are my friends.

RUTH Oh that is nice. Tell me about them.

PAULINE Well there is Ralph. He looked after me.

RUTH Yes. And?

PAULINE And David.

RUTH Who is David?

PAULINE	David is a man.
RUTH	A special man?
PAULINE	He likes weaving and knitting.
RUTH	Weaving?
PAULINE	Yes.
RUTH	Oh that is nice.
PAULINE	Yes. And there was Alf.
RUTH	Alf?
PAULINE	Yes. I don't like Alf always.
RUTH	Why ever not?
PAULINE	He is grumpy.
RUTH	Grumpy?
PAULINE	Yes. But.. but he likes flowers.
RUTH	Oh that is nice.
PAULINE	Yes. He can smell them a long way.
RUTH	Can he now?
PAULINE	Yes.

(pause)

(Pauline starts to cry)

PAULINE	Rachel didn't come today, she didn't.
RUTH	Who's Rachel?
PAULINE	My friend. My best friend.
RUTH	I don't know Rachel. Did she say she wouldcome?
PAULINE	Yes. (pause) She always comes. Every day. Every day I wait for her and every day she comes. I wait for her at the edge of the forest. At the end of the path, the windy path that goes through the forest. I wait for her there. I sit and gaze across the valley. I see the forest and the valley. I see the path and... and.... and the kestrel. (excitedly) The kestrel is always there. By the grassy outcrop at the forest edge. He is waiting. He is waiting patiently. Like me. I wait patiently there too. For my friend. Rachel. (pauses and then starts to cry) But Rachel didn't come today she didn't. I waited. The kestrel waited. The forest waited. But she didn't come. Not today.
RUTH	There. There.

PAULINE	I did so much want to see her.
RUTH	So Rachel is your best friend?
PAULINE	Yes.
RUTH	And she walks through the forest to see you every day.
PAULINE	Yes.
RUTH	And you meet her at the edge of the forest?
PAULINE	Yes.
RUTH	And you often watch the kestrel waiting at the edge of the forest?
PAULINE	Yes. (crying)

(pause) (Ralph enters)

RALPH	Hello, Ruth, and how is Pauline today?
RUTH	I think that she's fine. You are fine aren't you Pauline?
PAULINE	I am looking into the forest.
RUTH	Where is the forest, Pauline? Where is the forest?

(Lx fade to b/o)

THE END

Lightning Source UK Ltd.
Milton Keynes UK
UKHW020635110722
405680UK00009B/669

Three One-Act Plays
by
Graham Sessions

Published G Sessions, 5 Luxton Court, EX15 1FJ
Imprint: Blurb.co.uk
All rights reserved.
A licence to perform these plays must be obtained from the publisher by email: g.s.publishingbiz@gmail.com
This work is not to be copied by any means whatsoever.
If this work is not available from your bookseller, please contact the publisher.